OVERVIEW

Overview

What clinches a successful sale? Smooth talk, a warm smile, and a firm handshake might make a good first impression, but clever businesspeople are more concerned with the value you have to offer them. Making a mutually beneficial deal requires careful preparation before you start the negotiation process. Potential customers are more likely to buy from suppliers who understand their needs and have all requisite information at their fingertips.

A first step in negotiating successfully is understanding the difference between selling and negotiating. A sale is simply a transaction between seller and buyer, and is the result of closing a deal.

Negotiation, however, involves defining the terms of the deal – who gets what in exchange for what. A good negotiator will be able to work out the best possible deal with any given client and product.

Successful sales negotiations involve identifying and building on areas of agreement and they can help you build lasting, mutually beneficial relationships with customers.

In this book, you'll learn why it's important to use a systematic sales negotiation process, when it's relevant to use this process, and what the stages in the process are. You'll also learn more about the first stage in the process, which is preparing properly before negotiation begins.

An important activity in the preparation stage is to determine objectives for a negotiation – including yours and those of your customer.

Once you've done this, you can prepare the concessions you're willing to make in the book of negotiating. This involves weighing what you can afford to offer the other party against what you hope to get. In this book, you'll learn more about each of these activities and how to approach them.

Ultimately, this book will equip you to complete the first steps in making effective, long-lasting, and profitable sales agreements with your customers.

Consider a sales manager at a small graphic design company who's competing for projects with other design companies in the same city. Whenever he meets with a potential client, he names a higher price than his competitors and refuses to bargain. Needless to say, he fails to attract new clients and the design company goes out of business. The sales manager should have realized that successful sales negotiations are about give and take – or what's called the careful exchange of value.

By nature, a sales negotiation involves two parties with different goals trying to reach a mutually acceptable agreement.

Negotiation Skills for Sales Professionals

With good negotiation skills, you'll be able to facilitate this process and ensure you and the other party reach agreement. You'll also be able to influence the proceedings so that the outcome is more favorable to you than to your negotiation partner.

The four stages of the sales negotiation process are preparation, presentation, value exchange, and closing. This book focuses on value exchange. It covers the ways you can get the best possible deal for yourself because you'll know more about the what, when, and how of value exchange.

In this book, you'll learn strategies to ensure a desirable outcome from a value exchange and what concessions to offer to convince the other party to agree to the deal.

You'll also learn when to offer concessions. Poor timing can negatively affect the outcome of a negotiation. By learning how to best offer concessions, you'll be in a better position to negotiate the best possible deal and achieve your sales objectives.

A negotiation can be like a game of chess – you need to overcome problems and counter moves made against you in order to achieve your goal, which is to win the game. In sales, every negotiation's goal is to persuade your customers you're offering them good value, answer all their questions and respond to their objections, reach an agreement, and bring the meeting to a close.

During a negotiation, you may need to field questions and counter objections concerning your proposal at any point, not just in the middle or before closing.

It's clearly a good idea to have a well worked out negotiation plan and array of techniques ready so that any potential problems don't prevent you from reaching your goal.

In this book, you'll learn strategies to help instill a sense of trust in your client during a negotiation. When your client trusts you, this person will be more willing to share information with you and less suspicious of you.

You'll also learn to overcome interpersonal barriers in a negotiation. For example, how do you respond to a customer who just threatens to leave or makes extreme demands that you just can't accept?

And you'll learn how to recognize strategies that help you overcome a deadlock in a negotiation, such as making minor concessions and finding areas of possible agreement, while maintaining control over your emotions. This book will also allow you to practice your learned skills in a simulation in which you'll use negotiation strategies to overcome barriers and reach an agreement with your client.

CHAPTER 1 - PREPARING TO NEGOTIATE

CHAPTER 1 - Preparing to Negotiate
   SECTION 1 - The Sales Negotiation Process
   SECTION 2 - Determining Both Sides' Objectives
   SECTIONS 3 - Preparing Concessions

SECTION 1 - THE SALES NEGOTIATION PROCESS

SECTION 1 - The Sales Negotiation Process

The four-stage sales negotiation process – which consists of preparation, presentation, value exchange, and closing – helps ensure you prepare and deal with the complexities of sales negotiations properly. It also significantly improves the chances of reaching mutual agreement and developing important and lasting business relationships. You use this process when a potential deal involves more than one variable and when both parties have something of value to exchange with one another.

During the preparation stage, you need to establish your objectives and predict those of your negotiation partner. You then need to analyze the gap and develop your negotiation strategies accordingly. The presentation stage takes you through developing the agenda, establishing who has the authority to commit to a deal, presenting objectives and positions, and setting up a Q&A session. During the value exchange stage, you address deal breakers first and make concessions. Finally, during the closing stage, you ensure you've covered everything on the agenda, make adjustments, and finalize the agreement.

THE IMPORTANCE OF USING A PROCESS

The importance of using a process

Business in the 21st century is extremely competitive. A good sales pitch, charm, and a persuasive sales approach may not be enough to close the deal. Sales isn't just about promising the best product at the lowest price. It's about providing value and solutions, and developing relationships.

For these reasons, it's important to use a negotiation process that ensures proper preparation and provides a systematic method for exchanging value. This increases the chances of achieving agreement during the selling process.

Three characteristics of sales negotiations make it both necessary and beneficial to use a proper process:
- sales negotiations are often complicated,
- although they shouldn't be treated as arguments, sales negotiations are essentially adversarial, and
- sales negotiations tend to be time-consuming.

Complicated

Sales negotiations are complicated because they involve various details that have to be considered. Sales negotiations aren't just about discussing price. They're potentially complicated because they also involve negotiating important details such as licensing agreements, legal clauses, and intellectual property rights.

Taking a process-focused approach to sales negotiations helps you navigate through all these details and analyze the entire structure of a deal. It also involves preparing ahead of time and using a system to trade value, helping ensure you don't end up concluding deals that aren't in your favor.

Adversarial

Sales negotiations aren't arguments but they are adversarial by nature. They involve two or more parties competing to try to secure the best deal possible. However, compromise is crucial if negotiations are to succeed and result in win-win situations that all parties are happy with.

Using a systematic process to guide negotiations can help ensure that all parties reach agreement. It guides individuals through the bargaining stage, helping them avoid tension and develop long-lasting relationships.

Time-consuming

Salespeople often rush through sales negotiations in an attempt to close deals quickly. This can mean that they make various compromises that end up negatively affecting them and their companies.

It's important to remember that successful sales negotiations take time. Using a systematic process to negotiate forces you to work through the required stages patiently, instead of rushing and ending up with an unsatisfactory deal.

Question

Why is it beneficial to use a sales negotiation process?

Options:

1. It ensures you prepare adequately before entering negotiations
2. It enables you to conclude deals faster, which makes good business sense
3. It can help you build long-term relationships with customers
4. It ensures you don't rush through sales negotiations
5. It makes it unnecessary to waste time preparing beforehand for sales negotiations

Answer

Option 1: This option is correct. Given the complex nature of sales negotiations, success depends on preparing properly ahead of time and on systematically trading value with other parties. Following an established process can help ensure you do this.

Option 2: This option is incorrect. Rushing through sales negotiations can mean you end up making concessions that have a negative impact on you and your organization. Following a clear process helps ensure you don't do this.

Option 3: This is a correct option. A systematic process for sales negotiations focuses on creating mutual agreement between all parties. In turn, this helps the individuals involved to develop long-term relationships.

Option 4: This is a correct option. Rushing through sales negotiations can mean making compromises that you don't need to and that aren't in your favor. A sales negotiation process forces you to work through the required stages patiently.

Option 5: This is an incorrect option. It's always necessary to prepare beforehand for sales negotiations. Failing to do this can mean that you end up making unfavorable deals, or deals you aren't authorized to make or can't implement. Following an established process helps ensure you prepare properly.

WHEN TO USE A NEGOTIATION PROCESS

When to use a negotiation process

The sales negotiation process is typically used in two instances:
- when there's more than one variable to consider, and
- when both parties have something of value to exchange.

More than one variable

The sales negotiation process is useful when parties have to reach agreement on more than one variable, whether this is a tangible or an intangible item. Examples may be price, length of contract, and speed of delivery.

If two parties have to agree on just one variable – such as price – they're involved in haggling or bargaining, rather than negotiating.

Both parties have something to exchange

The sales negotiation process is used when each party has something of value to the other party to exchange.

For instance, a salesperson may offer a customer a free service plan and delivery in return for a bulk order. The customer may offer the salesperson free advertising on the customer's popular web site.

Say a garment manufacturer wants a supplier to deliver textiles within 24 hours of orders being placed, at a cheaper cost per yard than a competitor. In turn, the supplier hopes to secure a long-term contract and make a profit. In this case, it's relevant to use a sales negotiation process because each party has something of value to the other to exchange and multiple variables are involved.

However, if a supplier offers a manufacturer textiles at a price of $2 per yard and the manufacturer simply wants to get the price down to $1 per yard, it's just haggling – rather than negotiating – that's involved.

Question

Which sales situations require the use of a sales negotiation process?

Options:

1. A customer wants to purchase computer hardware and wants it delivered free of charge. A salesperson wants to make the sale and convince the customer to purchase an extended service plan.

2. A customer wants to purchase a vehicle for $1,500 less than the advertised price. The seller is willing to offer only a $900 reduction on the price.

3. A customer wants free advertising on a company web site. A salesperson wants a percentage of revenue generated from sales through the web site.

4. A customer with a set budget of $4,500 wants to purchase a training solution for two salespeople. A sales

consultant offers training for $3,000 for one employee, and a discounted $2,000 for a second.

Answer

Option 1: This option is correct. There's more than one variable in this instance – cost and profit – and both parties have something of value to offer one another.

Option 2: This option is incorrect. Only one variable is being considered in this situation – price. As such, this is simple bargaining, rather than negotiating.

Option 3: This is a correct option. In this sales situation, more than one variable is being considered – namely, advertising and revenue. Also, both parties have something of value to offer one another.

Option 4: This option is incorrect. Only one variable is being considered in this situation – price. As such, this is simple bargaining, rather than negotiating.

PREPARATION

Preparation

A sales negotiation process typically includes four stages – preparation, presentation, value exchange, and closing. Preparation is crucial because sales negotiations are complex and it's important that salespeople take the time to prepare adequately for the challenges negotiations present.

Proper preparation enables you to determine in advance what your strategy is going to be and how you're going to execute it. So it helps ensure that you can negotiate effectively.

To prepare effectively, you have to carry out certain activities during the preparation stage. You need to establish your objectives for the meeting, predict what your customer's objectives are, and analyze the gap between your objectives and those of your customer.

1. Establish your objectives

It's vital to determine exactly what your objectives are – or what it is you want to achieve on behalf of your company – through negotiation. This will prevent you from wasting time on negotiating about things that aren't important.

Objectives for a sales negotiation may relate to factors such as volume, price, length of contract, payment terms, and service.

2. Predict customer's objectives

To negotiate effectively, it's important to think about what your customer's objectives and needs are. Knowing this helps you align your strategy accordingly and avoid wasting time during the meeting.

It's also useful to know what your customers value so that you can better position what you have to offer.

3. Analyze the gap

Once you've determined your and your customer's objectives, you need to analyze the gap between these objectives. This involves identifying what you agree on and what you don't agree on. In any negotiation, there will be differences – but a good negotiator identifies these and develops strategies to deal with them.

PRESENTATION

Presentation

The second stage of the sales negotiation process is presentation. The first activity to complete during this stage is for both parties to agree on the agenda for a meeting.

A sales meeting agenda typically outlines the time, location, and duration of a meeting, and the names of meeting participants.

It also outlines negotiation points that are central to the meeting – such as terms of service, pricing, and conditions of a sale – and the order in which they'll be discussed.

In some cases, the agenda may specify whether additional people, such as financial counselors or senior executives, may accompany the parties due to attend the negotiations.

When creating an agenda, it's a good idea to place negotiation items that both parties are more likely to agree on at the top of the agenda, so that they're discussed first.

These items can be resolved easily, leaving the rest of the meeting to discuss the more complex items.

This will also help to set a positive tone for the meeting, because if the parties find it easy to resolve the initial items addressed, they're more likely to be ready to listen and compromise on the more difficult issues.

The second activity in the presentation stage is to establish each party's authority to commit to a deal. Often an individual has authority only up to a certain point. For instance, an organization's representative may be given the authority to sign an agreement that offers a discount up to, but no more than, 15%.

In the third activity in the presentation stage, both parties present their objectives and positions in relation to the negotiation points. It's important to understand the difference between objectives and positions.

Objectives

Objectives are the central aims of negotiation. They're constant. The parties involved may change their ideas about how their objectives can be met, but the objectives themselves won't change.

An example of an objective is to secure a signed contract for a minimum amount of $45,000 per year. The objective will stay the same even if the terms of the contract are adjusted.

Positions

A position is a defined stance or standpoint that's in keeping with a negotiator's interests. Unlike an objective, it may change during the course of a negotiation. In other words, individuals may be flexible about how their objectives are met, without compromising those objectives.

For example, one person's position may be that a contract worth $45,000 per annum should have a five-year term. During negotiation, however, this person may agree to a term of four years. Although the objective of securing a signed contract for $45,000 remains the same, the person's position has changed.

Presenting objectives and positions is a way for individuals to understand one another and identify areas of possible agreement and disagreement.

This activity is essential. Even if you've done your preparation, the other party may mention an objective or position that you hadn't anticipated – and you'll need to respond to this.

The final activity in the presentation stage is to set up a question and answer, or Q&A, session, also known as discovery time.

During the Q&A session, parties can ask and answer questions relating to all that's been discussed up to this point in the meeting. For example, they may ask questions about the objectives and positions that have been presented.

It can be useful to summarize and restate what's been discussed to ensure there are no misunderstandings. It's essential to remember that the main purpose of the Q&A session is to exchange vital information.

The questions you ask during this stage will help give you greater insight into the objectives and positions of your customer. It's also important that you listen actively to the information that's relayed to you.

During the presentation stage of the sales negotiation process, it's important not to discuss things you promised you wouldn't discuss when you asked for a meeting. Also, at this stage, you won't be negotiating or selling yet. Instead, this is a time for both parties to present their needs, objectives, and positions, and to exchange as much information as possible.

Question

What objectives should you meet during the presentation stage of the sales negotiation process?

Options:

1. Determine what you and your customer want to achieve

2. Agree on the main issues to discuss and the order in which to discuss them

3. Ensure all parties have an opportunity to present their objectives and positions

4. Consider the gap between your objectives and those of your negotiation partner

5. Determine what authority your customer – or the customer's representative – has to commit to a deal

Answer

Option 1: This option is incorrect. At the presentation stage, you and the customer state what your objectives are. You don't determine what you want to achieve.

Option 2: This is a correct option. During the presentation stage, it's important that both parties agree on an agenda for the meeting. The agenda will list the main issues that need to be discussed. It should start with the simple issues – those that parties are likely to agree on – and then move to the more complex ones.

Option 3: This option is correct. During the presentation stage, all parties should present their objectives and positions. This involves exchanging information rather than participating in actual negotiations.

Option 4: This is an incorrect option. To prepare for a negotiation meeting, you should analyze the gap between your objectives and those of your negotiation partner during the preparation stage. You don't do this during the presentation stage.

Option 5: This is a correct option. Parties determine each other's level of authority to commit to an agreement during the presentation stage of the sales negotiation process.

Lila works for a company of marketing consultants. She sets up a meeting with Corbin, a manager at a newly established restaurant, who wants to work with her to boost the restaurant's profile and thus increase the number of customers. Lila prepares for the meeting by doing some research on the restaurant, what it offers, how it's been marketed up to this point, and what its client base is.

After doing her research and determining what it is she can offer Corbin, Lila sets the objective of securing a signed contract for $105,000 by the end of the meeting.

She also considers an acceptable alternative to this objective, which is a signed contract for $95,000 in return for limited consulting services related to advertising – which is what Corbin is most concerned with.

Follow along as Lila enters the presentation stage and meets with Corbin.

Lila: I've done some research into your restaurant's needs, and I think I can help you. The most important thing for you is advertising – is that right?

Corbin: Correct. Advertising is important, as are some other issues I think we should discuss today.

Lila: Well, I don't think we need to bother with an agenda or anything formal like that. The main point of discussion is how to boost your restaurant's profile using advertising.

Lila is indifferent.

Corbin: OK, if you say so. Essentially, I want to increase the number of customers I have dining in my restaurant.

Lila: It's our aim to help you with that. Besides using traditional, print media advertising, we'll focus on increasing your brand exposure, market share, and web site traffic.

Corbin: That sounds good. Those are areas I didn't even think about. Lila: They're important considerations these days. We can offer our assistance in all these areas for a fee of $105,000.

Corbin: $105,000...well, it has cost me a lot to get this restaurant up and running. My main objective currently is...

Corbin is concerned.

Lila: We can improve your current marketing strategy and provide plans on how to best proceed to increase your bottom line. If it's just traditional advertising you want to focus on though, we'd be willing to handle that for $95,000.

Corbin: Yes, but my position on this is that...

Corbin is frustrated.

Lila: The important thing right now is determining whether we have an agreement, so we can get started.

Question

The presentation stage of the sales negotiation process includes various activities.

Which activity did Lila carry out effectively?
Options:
1. She agreed with Corbin on an agenda
2. She presented her objectives and positions
3. She established what authority Corbin had to commit to an agreement
4. She allowed Corbin to present his objectives and positions
5. She included discovery time in the meeting

Answer

Option 1: This option is incorrect. Lila didn't agree on an agenda with Corbin. As a result, their conversation wasn't focused and they didn't discuss any of the possible negotiation points.

Option 2: This is the correct option. Lila was clear about how her company can assist Corbin's restaurant. She outlined two possible deals – for $105,000 and $95,000 respectively.

Option 3: This is an incorrect option. At no point in the discussion did Lila determine Corbin's authority to commit to a contract or an agreement. As a result, she may discover too late that Corbin doesn't have the authority to make a final decision.

Option 4: The option is incorrect. Lila presented her objectives and positions, but didn't give Corbin an opportunity to present his. This kept her from learning about the potential client and prevented the meeting from being a success.

Option 5: This is an incorrect option. Lila has yet to hold a Q&A session, which is the discovery time during which parties ask and answer questions to gather more information.

Up to this point, the only thing Lila has done effectively is to set out her own objectives and positions.

Noticing Corbin's frustration, Lila continues through the presentation stage, allowing for discovery time by opening the discussion up for questions and answers.

Because Lila neglected to involve Corbin in a meaningful way earlier in the sales presentation, they don't reach an agreement, and Corbin concludes the meeting by saying he'll be in contact with Lila once he's met with another marketing consultancy.

VALUE EXCHANGE

Value exchange

Unfortunately, Lila won't have an opportunity to continue on to the third stage of the sales negotiation process – the value exchange.

This is when actual negotiation occurs. Both parties attempt to reach agreement, while trying to ensure their own objectives are fully met.

During this stage, you need to establish areas of agreement and disagreement, and then focus on resolving any disagreement. Some points of disagreement are less important than others, and it's up to you to decide which to prioritize. It's always best to address deal breakers first to avoid wasting time. A deal breaker is any sticking point, or term, that one of the parties in a negotiation absolutely requires.

Resolving disagreements requires you to bargain, or make concessions. During this process, one party may propose a concession. The other party responds by making that concession conditional. This process continues until a final agreement is reached.

For example, negotiation partners can't agree on the discount that the customer should receive on the unit price. The customer wants 10%, but the supplier refuses. So the customer offers a concession by increasing the order by 7,000 units. The supplier responds with an offer of a 5% discount provided the customer orders 10,000 more units.

Once all the parties reach a final agreement, you can enter the final stage of the sales negotiation process – closing.

CLOSING

Closing

Closing is a crucial stage during which you review what has been discussed. You also use this time to ensure you understand each other and have an agreement. As closing activities, the parties should compare what they've discussed to what was included on the agenda, make any necessary adjustments, and finalize the agreement.

Compare to agenda

It's good practice in the closing stage to review each of the agenda items to ensure they've been dealt with and agreed upon.

Make adjustments

Before accepting the final agreement, one or both parties may need to make certain adjustments. You should ensure everyone agrees to these and is satisfied with the outcome.

Finalize the agreement

Once all parties have reviewed the agreement, summarized it, and are happy with its terms and conditions, they can move on to finalizing it. This may involve signing a contract or writing up a memorandum of understanding.

Question

Match the stages of the sales negotiation process with their corresponding activities.

Options:

A. Closing
B. Preparation
C. Value exchange
D. Presentation

Targets:

1. Compare the final agreement to the items that made up the sales meeting agenda

2. Determine what strategy you'll use to secure agreement during a negotiation meeting

3. Identify and resolve areas of disagreement by making necessary concessions

4. Establish what authority each party has to commit to an agreement

Answer

During the closing stage of the sales negotiation process, both parties should ensure they've covered all points on the agenda. They should then make any necessary adjustments and finalize their agreement.

During the preparation stage, you should determine how you're going to approach a sales negotiation and what strategy you're going to use to secure a deal.

During the value exchange stage, both parties need to focus on resolving any areas of disagreement through bargaining.

During the presentation stage, it's important to establish each party's authority to commit to a deal or contract.

SECTION 2 - DETERMINING BOTH SIDES' OBJECTIVES

SECTION 2 - Determining Both Sides' Objectives

A sales negotiation is successful if both parties agree that what they've received is of greater value than what they've given. So objectives for a sales meeting should focus on securing agreement terms that maximize value.

Your objectives for a sales meeting should be influenced by the purpose of the meeting, what you know about the customer, your relationship with the customer, and your personal sales goals.

You can use sources like previous conversations, briefings from others in your organization, and customer queries to help anticipate the customer's objectives.

CURRENCY AND VALUE

Currency and value

For a sales negotiation to have a successful outcome – for both you and your customer – you need to prepare an informed presentation beforehand. The first steps to doing this are to determine your objectives and accurately predict your customer's objectives for the sales meeting.

The objectives you set for a sales negotiation depend on two important concepts – value and currency.

Value

The value of a sales agreement is the benefit you obtain from what the other party has to trade. It may be a financial benefit or relate to other types of benefits, like saving time or even improving your self-image.

Currency

Currency refers to what you have to trade – or what terms of agreement you have to offer in return for the value you hope to obtain.

In a good trade, both parties consider the currency they receive to be of greater value than the currency they trade.

Say an accounting company pays a group of IT technicians a monthly fee to provide technical support and resolve any networking problems that may arise. The technicians' service is worth more to the company than the fee it pays because it prevents potentially expensive disruptions to its daily operations.

To the technicians, the monthly payment they receive from the accounting company is more valuable than the services they provide – or it wouldn't be feasible for them to offer these services.

The point at which the value to you of what you have to give up is greater than the customer's offer is called your walk-away point. For example, if the IT technicians ask for an exorbitant fee for their services, the accounting company would no longer consider it worth negotiating for those services. Similarly, the IT technicians won't consider dropping the price of their services below a certain point, or they won't obtain value from the agreement.

Question

How is the concept of value defined in relation to the objectives for a sales negotiation?

Options:

1. The benefit you can gain through successful negotiation

2. The cost to each party of obtaining a desired result

3. The financial worth of what you hope to gain

Answer

Option 1: This is the correct option. All objectives for a sales negotiation relate to obtaining value, which can be defined as the benefit you can gain from what the other party has to exchange.

Option 2: This is an incorrect option. The concept of value is about perceived gain. It refers to the benefit you can gain from what another party has to exchange, rather than to the cost of obtaining this benefit.

Option 3: This is an incorrect option. The value you assign to what the other party has to trade will shape your objectives. However, the value isn't necessarily financial. For example, it may be a value derived from the convenience of a service or even from the social status associated with owning a particular product.

You derive value by setting the right agreement terms for a sale – or put another way, by ensuring the value of what you agree to give is lower than the value to your company of what you'll get in exchange. Some examples of agreement terms relate to profit margin, product volume, use of company resources, the warranty associated with a sale, and payment terms.

Profit margin

The higher the profit margin you secure through a deal, the greater the financial worth of the deal to your company. For example, if you sell four photocopiers at more than cost price, your company benefits financially.

Product volume

You may be able to increase the value of a deal to your company by increasing the product volume involved. Incentives like discounts for bulk purchases may help secure this type of agreement. For example, if you can sell office stationery at a good price by giving the buyer extra volume, you should do so.

Use of company resources

The extent to which your company uses its resources may affect the value of an agreement. So you can increase value by reducing the drain on resources. For example, an IT company requests 24/7 dedicated support once it's bought your company's technology. However, your company may not be able to absorb the drain on resources as a result of this request. The deal may be more valuable to you if you can agree on 12-hour-per-day support instead.

Warranty

Warranty terms refer to how much cover or support your warranty will contain for the customer's purchase and the warranty period itself. For example, if you want to sell a new accounting software package, the deal can be made significantly more valuable if you sell it with a one-year, instead of a three-year, warranty.

Payment terms

Favorable payment terms can increase the value of a deal to your company – for example if your company can pay in installments, or even delay payments.

Question

Which agreement terms add value to the proposed sales deals?

Options:

1. Selling a $1,000 photocopier for $800 plus maintenance servicing

2. Selling a computer for $300 below cost

3. Offering a two-year guarantee on parts in exchange for a higher purchase price

4. Selling equipment at a lower-than-cost price but adding maintenance services

5. Selling printing paper in bulk at a slightly discounted price

6. Agreeing to allow the customer to pay in installments for a big purchase

7. Granting access to your databases

Answer

Option 1: This is a correct option. Offering ongoing maintenance servicing for the product is a way to make up and increase the financial value of a discounted deal. It also carries the potential for securing more deals with the same customer.

Option 2: This is an incorrect option. Selling an item below cost with no concessions doesn't represent value.

Option 3: This is a correct option. The deal becomes more valuable to the seller if the warranty can be offset by a higher purchase price.

Option 4: This option is incorrect. There is no value to selling for less and still offering company services.

Option 5: This option is correct. Increasing the product volume of a deal often also increases its value.

Option 6: This is a correct option. Value can be added to a deal with flexible payment terms, such as delayed payment or installment payments.

Option 7: This option is correct. The use of a company's resources can add value to a sales deal.

PREPARING YOUR OBJECTIVES

Preparing your objectives

When identifying the objectives for a sales negotiation, you need to ensure they represent value to both you and your customer.

Your objectives for a sales meeting will depend largely on three factors:
- the purpose of the meeting,
- who the customer is, and
- the nature of your relationship with the customer.

Purpose of meeting

A potential customer who's currently doing business with your competitor but is shopping for a better price may ask to meet with you. You may contact someone and ask to meet so you can determine whether there's the potential to do business. Or you may already know the potential for good business exists, so you meet to present your offer.

Your objectives should vary accordingly. For example, if the purpose of setting up a meeting is to establish a potential for doing business, your objectives are to get to know the customer and how you could meet the customer's requirements.

Customer

The nature of the customer, and the customer's needs and buying preferences, should influence your objectives.

Say you market a range of investment products. Your objectives for meeting with a potential client who's in her 60s and has retired will probably differ from those for a meeting with a couple in their 30s with young children. Characteristics of the customers will affect the products you aim to sell and what you aim to discuss.

In the case of a potential business-to-business deal, the nature of the customer's business and industry may determine standard prices, typical time frames, and other terms that form part of your objectives.

Relationship

The nature of your relationship with a customer should help determine your objectives.

For example, if you're meeting with someone you haven't met before, your objectives may include building rapport and gathering information. If you're meeting with a long-standing customer whose needs and preferences you know well, your objectives will be more focused – perhaps upgrading the customer's existing contract or securing a purchase of a new product offering.

Your personal sales goals will also influence your objectives for a sales meeting. For example, your goal may be to make $60,000 in sales for the month, discuss at least three out of five key products during the meeting, close a deal, or arrange a date for a follow-up meeting.

Lucinda works as a sales lead for a multinational high-tech consultancy. She has a meeting with Mabel, the vice president of development for a wireless device company.

Mabel's company has been receiving negative customer comments because of weaknesses in its devices, including their failure to work properly across different platforms. So Mabel wants Lucinda's consultancy to help with the design and interoperability of the devices, and to assist the company with its marketing efforts.

Lucinda assesses the needs of Mabel's company and then sets her objective for a sales meeting as securing a signed contract for $140,000.

Because it's a new relationship, she sets an objective of fostering good ties between the two companies, as well as of securing a contract to address the interoperability of the company's devices.

Question

Frank, an IT consultant, is meeting with a longstanding customer, Danny, whose organization develops new software and needs expert assistance. Frank knows Danny's company pays well. He calculates the new project's cost of $147,000 for seven weeks' work, if Danny takes the full package.

What are appropriate objectives for Frank to set for the meeting?

Options:

1. Have Danny sign the full $147,000 contract
2. Introduce products outside the technology range
3. Introduce some new technology products
4. Get Danny to agree to the $147,000 contract and then try to increase it to $150,000
5. Upgrade a contract with Danny's company

Answer

Option 1: This is a correct option. Frank should enter the meeting with the purpose of getting Danny to accept the full fee on the seven-week project.

Option 2: This is an incorrect option. Frank should only pitch products relevant to his customer.

Option 3: This is a correct option. Knowing Danny's organization is a buyer of technology-related solutions, Frank should try to offer related products.

Option 4: This is an incorrect option. Frank shouldn't plan to alienate a customer with a cheap attempt at raising the fee after an agreement.

Option 5: This is a correct option. Frank should try to build on the business relationship between the two companies to expand business.

DETERMINING CUSTOMER OBJECTIVES

Determining customer objectives

As well as defining your objectives for a sales meeting, you should predict the customer's objectives. If you've anticipated the customer's goals and know what the customer values, you'll be better equipped to preempt counterarguments to any proposals you make.

Sources you can use to help determine the customer's objectives include previous conversations, briefings from others in your organization, and customer queries.

Previous conversations

Previous conversations with the customer – possibly from your first contact – can provide information about what the customer wants, expects, and may insist upon.

For example, if a customer enquires about top-of-the-range products in an initial telephone call, you'll know that one of the customer's objectives is to secure the best product available in the relevant industry.

Briefings

The briefing from others in your organization about which products or services to promote contains useful background research.

For example, on a lead generation form, you find notes that indicate the customer is probably interested in cell phone software accessories. The form also contains other relevant background information about the company's location and the size of its sales force.

Customer queries

Customer queries and feedback from sources like customer web sites, social networking, and trade show contacts can yield valuable information. By noting how your customers' clientele are reacting, you can gather what your customers' objectives might be.

For example, if it's common for customers to compare a company unfavorably to its competitors, you can deduce that an objective for the company is to become more competitive.

Lucinda knows from her first conversation with Mabel that Mabel's company wants to improve the design and interoperability of its devices. So she knows that one of the customer's objectives will be to improve the quality of its products.

However, Lucinda delves further by consulting a briefing document. The background research section clearly indicates that other objectives might be to improve sales and capture a wider share of the market.

Finally, Lucinda visits Mabel's company web site and notices postings from customers who are unhappy with the quality of the company's products. Based on what she reads, she knows Mabel would want to add the repair of the company's damaged reputation as a likely objective.

When preparing for a sales negotiation, remember that the best objectives are ones in which both you and the customer can find value. It's these types of objectives that set a positive tone in a sales meeting, lead to the best results, and foster long-term relationships.

Question

Danny has told Frank that his software development company wants to expand, with the help of Frank's IT consultancy. Frank notes that on the Internet, many customers rate this company unfavorably in comparison to its competitors. In addition, Frank learns from a colleague that Danny's company is hoping to get the new software to market before a competitor finishes developing a similar software.

What are Danny's objectives likely to be, based on what is of value to him and his company?

Options:

1. Secure the largest share of the market
2. Increase its competitiveness
3. Maintain ties with Frank's IT consultancy
4. Get Frank's services at the lowest cost, no matter what
5. Drive up his company's sales and profitability

Answer

Option 1: This is a correct option. A briefing suggests Danny's company wants the new software to be developed quickly, probably because it wants to capture a share of the market before a competitor does.

Option 2: This is a correct option. In response to the many unfavorable comparisons on its web site, it's reasonable to suppose that Danny's company would want to become more competitive.

Option 3: This option is incorrect. Developing a long-term relationship is more likely to be one of Frank's, rather than Danny's, objectives.

Option 4: This is an incorrect option. It's more likely that Danny will aim to improve product quality, even if it means paying a little more than necessary.

Option 5: This is a correct option. Danny's company wants to expand, so one of its objectives is likely to be an increase in sales and profits.

SECTION 3 - PREPARING CONCESSIONS

SECTION 3 - Preparing Concessions

Once you've determined your and your customer's objectives for a sales negotiation, you should determine what concessions you can make and how valuable each of these is. You can do this by establishing a range of acceptable values for each objective, identifying concessions based on these, and then ranking the concessions.

STEPS FOR PREPARING CONCESSIONS

Steps for preparing concessions

Once you've prepared your own objectives and anticipated the customer's objectives for a sales meeting, it's time to consider how you'll approach the negotiation process. To do this, you need to examine the objectives, determine where potential problems may arise, and prepare a strategy for making concessions during the value exchange stage of the meeting.

A concession is anything you're willing to trade to get something back that's of more value to you.

A simple example of a concession is a manufacturer arranging earlier delivery – for example, on Tuesday instead of Friday – if the customer buys a larger quantity of a product.

It's important to prepare a set of concessions you're willing to make before you meet so you're clear about what you should and shouldn't agree to during the negotiation process. To do this, you can perform two key activities:

- determine a range of acceptable agreement terms – from least to most desirable – for each of your objectives, and
- list and then rank the concessions you're willing to make, based on the ranges you identified.

DETERMINING RANGES

Determining ranges

For each objective you've identified, you should determine the least and the most you're willing to accept. This gives you a range so you can be flexible during the negotiation process, without unintentionally giving away more than you want to – or more than your company has authorized you to.

Using definite values – or metrics – to quantify the range for each objective helps clarify exactly what you're willing to agree to.

The metrics you use can vary. They may be monetary values, days or hours, or percentages.

For instance, you might plan to offer a discount between 5% and 10%, or you may be authorized to agree on a price between $20,000 and $25,000.

To help determine the range of acceptable terms for each objective, you should identify the high point of the range, the low point, and your walk-away point.

High point

The high point of a range is what your opening offer will be and reflects the best possible outcome for you. It shouldn't, however, be excessive. It has to be a value you can justify as reasonable using objective criteria or information gathered through research.

Low point

As you negotiate and offer concessions, you'll move closer to your low point, which is the minimum you're willing to settle for. Although this value will be lower than the one you've determined is optimal, it's still acceptable to you.

Walk-away point

Your walk-away point is anything below the lowest value you've decided to accept. So anything below this is unacceptable. It's the point at which you'll "walk away" from the negotiation if there's no agreement.

Lucinda, the sales lead for a multinational, high-tech consultancy, is preparing to meet with Mabel, the vice president of an established wireless device company that's a key prospective client. One of Lucinda's objectives for the meeting is to secure a contract at a good price. She needs to decide on the high, low, and walk-away points for this objective.

High point

Lucinda's high point, or ideal outcome, is to secure $140,000 for a contract to assist Mabel's company with marketing, as well as the design and operability of its wireless devices.

She can justify this price because her company has done similar work for other clients within the same price range. Also, through research, Lucinda has determined that Mabel's company is in desperate need of assistance to improve both its products and its reputation.

Low point

Lucinda's low point is $95,000 for a contract to assist Mabel's company only with the design and operability of its wireless devices. The contract will exclude any marketing advice.

Walk-away point

Lucinda's walk-away point is anything below her low point of $95,000 for a contract.

By determining the high point of the range, Lucinda establishes what her opening offer will be at the start of the negotiation. If Mabel's not happy with this, Lucinda can continue making concessions – up to accepting a contract for $95,000, Lucinda's low point.

She knows that she won't offer anything below her low point. However, based on the range she's set, Lucinda may then identify other appropriate types of concessions that she's willing to make.

If Mabel doesn't accept the opening offer, Lucinda's first concession is to offer in-kind services, such as administrative assistance, the use of phones and Internet connections, and the use of office space at any of her consultancy's international branches. If Mabel asks for more, she'll offer interoperability research. Her last option will be to drop the interoperability portion of the work and try to sell Mabel on the $95,000 contract for helping with device production.

Question

Frank is preparing for a sales negotiation with a prospective client, Danny. How should Frank use the range values he has determined during the negotiation?

Options:

1. He should decrease the price to $125,000 if Danny doesn't accept higher offers

2. He should open with an offer of a contract for $147,000

3. He should open with an offer of a contract for $130,000

4. He should offer price concessions, but stop at $130,000

Answer

Option 1: This option is incorrect. The low point of the range Frank identified is $130,000. Any price below this represents his walk-away point.

Option 2: This option is correct. The high point of Frank's range is $147,000, so this should be his opening offer.

Option 3: This is an incorrect option. The low point of the range Frank identified is $130,000. This is the lowest price he should consider accepting, rather than his ideal price, which is the one he should offer first.

Option 4: This is a correct option. If Danny isn't happy with the opening offer, Frank can gradually move closer to the lowest price he has decided is acceptable, which is $130,000.

RANKING CONCESSIONS

Ranking concessions

Once you've defined ranges for your objectives, you'll have a better idea of what concessions you're willing to make. You can then move on to the second key activity, which is to rank these concessions according to how valuable they are to you.

To do this effectively, first compare your list of objectives with the customer's objectives. This will give you a better idea of what's valuable to both of you, and of what your customer's concessions are mostly likely to be. You can then assign a rating to each concession. A simple approach is to assign each concession a rating of 1, 2, or 3, based on its value to you.

1 - Concessions that are most likely to be agreed on quickly during a negotiation should get a rating of 1. These are concessions you feel can be traded easily because they're of the least value to you.

Because these concessions are the items you and the customer will agree on easily, you should deal with them first during the meeting. You can then focus on dealing with more difficult concessions.

2 - Concessions that aren't likely to be sources of major disagreement can be assigned a rating of 2.

Concessions that are assigned a rating of 2 are not of the least value to you, but they're also not of the most value. They can be dealt with after concessions with a rating of 1, or later on in the negotiation process.

3 - You should give a rating of 3 to concessions that are of most value to you and that are likely sources of disagreement. These are the concessions you don't want to make, but may have to make if all else fails.

These are also the items of main concern to individuals, and may be deal-breakers. It's important to decide how to handle these and what you're willing to trade in order to achieve your objectives.

Consider Lucinda again. She reviews her objectives and Mabel's. She then considers her concessions – offering in-kind services, office space, and interoperability research, and suggesting they drop the interoperability portion of the work. She then ranks each.

In-kind services and office space

Lucinda rates the offer of in-kind services and office space as 1 because this would not cost her much. These are therefore highly tradable concessions and are concessions that Mabel is likely to agree to.

Interoperability research

The interoperability research is worth more to Lucinda than the in-kind services and office space, because her company's already invested in the research and it has additional value as it can directly help Mabel's company improve its products. Therefore Lucinda assigns this concession a rating of 2 – it's not the cheapest concession, but it's also not the most expensive.

Drop interoperability

Lucinda rates dropping the interoperability portion of the work at 3, because it's the most valuable concession and could be the biggest point of disagreement.

Offering this concession means a much lower contract price, which is why this is Lucinda's highest value concession, and it's something she doesn't want to offer unless all else fails.

Once you've identified ranges for your objectives, established concessions, and ranked these concessions, you've prepared properly for a sales negotiation. You can then proceed with confidence to the next stage of the sales negotiation process, when you and the customer meet and make your presentations.

Question

Consider Frank, who's preparing for a meeting with Danny and has created a list of concessions. How should Frank rank the concessions he has identified?

Options:

1. He should rank the offer of free 24/7 support as 3

2. He should rank the concession to advertise Danny's company logo as 2

3. He should rank the concession to offer free, continuous quarterly performance reviews as 1

4. He should rank the concession to offer a contract price of $130,000 as 3

5. He should rank the concession to lower the contract price to $130,000 and extend the completion time as 1

Answer

Option 1: This option is incorrect. This concession should be ranked as 1 because it's of the least value to Frank and both parties are likely to agree to it readily.

Option 2: This option is correct. Frank is probably not eager to give away free advertising, so that should not be in his first set of concessions. He should give it a rating of 2.

Option 3: This option is correct. This concession is one that Danny will most likely have no problem agreeing with, and it's of low value to Frank. It should therefore be assigned a rating of 1.

Option 4: This is a correct option. This concession is of the greatest value to Frank and is something he'll want to avoid offering unless all other concessions fail. So it should be given a rating of 3.

Option 5: This is an incorrect option. This concession is of high value to Frank and is something he'll want to avoid offering if he can. So it should be assigned a rating of 3.

CHAPTER 2 - VALUE EXCHANGE

CHAPTER 2 - Value Exchange
   SECTION 1 - What Concessions to Offer
   SECTION 2 - When to Offer Concessions
   SECTION 3 - How to Offer Concessions

SECTION 1 - WHAT CONCESSIONS TO OFFER

SECTION 1 - What Concessions to Offer

In a sales negotiation, the value exchange process involves trading concessions with the aim of reaching a mutually beneficial agreement. The benefits of using a value exchange approach are that this helps foster long-term relationships with your customers, maximizes outcomes for both parties, and enhances your image as someone who's reasonable, fair, and empathetic.

The best concessions are those that are inexpensive for you but of high value to the other party. To help determine what concessions you can offer, you should consider all the variables in a negotiation, determine what both you and the other party need, and then consider how you can both add value to the deal.

BENEFITS OF THE VALUE EXCHANGE APPROACH

Benefits of the value exchange approach

The real estate developer and businessman, Donald Trump, once stated "If you have what the other guy wants, you have a deal." In a sales negotiation, value exchange is the process of trading concessions and making compromises. Ideally it should result in terms that are beneficial for both parties – so both parties walk away with what they want.

Concessions are a valuable tool if you need to break an impasse, win a corresponding concession, conclude the agreement, or motivate the other party to change a position.

Every sales negotiation has a unique purpose and this will influence the approach you should use. For example, your approach should vary based on whether it's more important to secure the best outcome or to build a strong, long-term relationship with a customer. There are four typical approaches that each party can adopt during the negotiation process – competing, avoiding, accommodating, or compromising.

Competing

Competing is an aggressive approach. You focus on securing the best outcome for yourself, without considering the future state of your relationship with the customer. In this scenario, one party wins and the other party loses.

Avoiding

Avoiding is a negative approach that involves withdrawing from active negotiation. In this scenario, both parties lose because agreement isn't possible when one party refuses to engage actively in the negotiation process.

Accommodating

Accommodating is a defensive approach. You back off from achieving your direct goals so you can benefit from an ongoing relationship. In this scenario, you intentionally lose the negotiation to win in terms of a relationship.

Compromising

Compromising involves attempting to reach the best possible outcome while also building or maintaining a good relationship. Both parties are willing to enter a process of value exchange – that is, finding common ground and making concessions.

Compromising is the ideal approach because it involves basing agreements on a mutually beneficial exchange of value. The benefits of an approach based on value exchange are that this can help foster long-term relationships with your customers, maximize outcomes for both parties, and enhance your image as someone who's fair, reasonable, considerate, and empathetic.

Lucinda works as a sales lead for a multi-national high-tech consultancy. She's engaged in negotiations with Mabel, who wants to improve sales at the wireless device company she represents. Lucinda aims to secure a contract to the value of $140,000, but Mabel has just stated her company's financial situation and remarked that she almost certainly won't be able to agree to any price over $100,000.

In her response, Lucinda has the option of adopting a competing, avoiding, accommodating, or compromising negotiation approach.

Competing

"Mabel, you have to weigh up the short-term costs of getting your problems resolved immediately against the long-term losses you'll notice if you delay finding a solution. Unfortunately, there's no way to do the work you're asking for at any discounted price – the price is non-negotiable."

Avoiding

"Oh ... OK. Well, let's not talk about that now. Tell me more about the new product range you're developing and what you think are its strongest marketing points."

Accommodating

"OK. I'm sure we can meet that price. I'll probably need to chat with my supervisor first, but I don't think she'll mind, given that we have such a long-standing business relationship."

Compromising

"I don't think it's in the best interest of your company to delay implementing a solution, but unfortunately it's just not feasible for us to do the work you're asking for at the price you're proposing. We could come down slightly in price, but we might need to reduce the length or scope of the contract."

Each of Lucinda's four responses is an example of a particular negotiation approach.

In the example of a competing approach, Lucinda makes it clear that the price isn't negotiable and reinforces her position by making Mabel aware that a delay will harm Mabel's company. Lucinda takes an aggressive approach in which she's more concerned about the outcome than the relationship.

In the example of an avoiding approach, Lucinda stops engaging Mabel on the price issue by postponing it indefinitely and changing the subject. Her negative approach makes it very difficult to come to an agreement and the more likely result is that both parties will lose out in the process.

In the example of an accommodating approach, Lucinda gives in and offers Mabel no resistance to her low offer. Lucinda takes a defensive approach and backs off from achieving her goals for the sake of the relationship.

In the example of the compromising approach, Lucinda is realistic about what the asking price needs to be if the project is going to be worthwhile for her company. At the same time, she's empathetic to Mabel's situation and looks for ways to add more value to what they are able to offer Mabel within the existing price frame. She's offering Mabel savings in other areas.

Question

What are the benefits of the value exchange approach to sales?

Options:

1. Fostering long-term relationships with your customers by building real business value
2. Maximizing outcomes for both parties
3. Enhancing your image as someone who's reasonable, fair, and empathetic
4. Manipulating clients into agreeing to your terms while letting them think they're in control
5. Increasing your personal network of contacts in the industry

Answer

Option 1: This is a correct option. If you focus on exchanging value – instead of only on trying to "win" a negotiation or to placate the other party – you make it likely that both parties will reach a mutually beneficial agreement. This can help you build and maintain long-term relationships.

Option 2: This option is correct. If you focus on exchanging value – instead of achieving your goals at all costs – you're more likely to reach an agreement that offers maximum benefit for both parties.

Option 3: This is a correct option. If you focus on exchanging value with the aim that both parties should benefit from the outcomes, you'll earn a reputation as someone desirable to do business with.

Option 4: This option is incorrect. The value exchange process isn't an underhanded attempt to achieve your own objectives. Rather it's committed to achieving your own goals in a spirit of consideration and fairness toward your negotiating partner.

Option 5: This is an incorrect option. Although good relationships with your clients may lead them to introduce you to other potential clients, this isn't a direct benefit of the value exchange process.

APPROPRIATE CONCESSIONS

Appropriate concessions

To participate effectively in the value-exchange process, you need to identify the viable concessions. Some salespeople make the mistake of thinking price is the only issue in a sales meeting when there are other negotiable variables that can be just as important. Taking the time to consider all the variables that surround each negotiation gives you the best chance of maximizing outcomes.

Variables in a sales negotiation can be either tangible or intangible. For example, tangible variables may relate to money, people, or facilities. Intangible variables may relate to priorities, information, recognition and rewards, proprietary agreements, or mitigation of risks.

Money

Parties in a negotiation may offer concessions related to price – or a range of other types of concessions that have a financial impact. Examples are discounts for bulk purchases, lower rates with a longer-term contract, and extended payment terms.

People

People variables refer to the staff members, or the skills and abilities of your employees, that you can offer in assistance to the client. For example, you could offer to loan some of your staff members, technical support, or administrative help.

Facilities

Facility variables are the facilities that you have at your disposal that can be used as a solution to meet a client's particular need, and thereby increase your value contribution in the negotiation. For example, you might have additional space that could solve a client's storage problem.

Priorities

Priority variables refer to the level of importance or urgency you're willing to attribute to a client's situation. For example, you might be willing to accelerate an installation or delivery, or agree to a longer- or shorter-term contract.

Information

Information variables are the expertise and knowledge you have at your disposal that could be of benefit to your client. For example, this could be your knowledge of the industry, your network of contacts, or your ability to serve as a reference.

Recognition and rewards

Recognition and reward variables refer to the means you have of increasing your clients public status, image, or exposure. Examples include awarding "official vendor" status, the opportunity to present at a high profile conference, or joint advertising.

Proprietary agreements

Proprietary agreement variables are the specific ways that you can give your clients an advantage over their competition. For example, you might grant them first access to a new product or exclusive agreements.

Mitigation of risks

Mitigation of risk variables refer to the ways you're able to minimize any actual or perceived risk that your client might be concerned about. For example, you could provide a guaranteed escalating price structure, or offer product warranties and guarantees.

There are various questions you can ask to help identify concessions: What are the tangible and intangible variables?

What does the other party need that I can offer? What do I need that the other party can offer? How can we both add value to the deal?

What are the variables?

Lucinda identifies the primary variables as price, and the length and scope of the contract. There might also be a time-related variable if the company needs something done by a particular deadline.

What does the other party need?

Lucinda knows Mabel's company needs to do some damage control to counter its recent bad publicity about incompatibility issues for many of its wireless devices. Mabel's company may have to shut down many of its international-based offices to cut costs if a solution isn't implemented quickly.

What do I need?

Lucinda needs to walk away with a deal for $125,000 or more. Her company also needs to upgrade its in-office wireless devices.

How can we add value?

Lucinda knows she can trade off her company's foreign-based office space to help Mabel's company with its offshore office problems. She can also offer to do wireless device research, which might help Mabel's company fill some knowledge gaps. Lucinda would be willing to consider receiving additional wireless devices and support to partially compensate for a reduced price.

The best concessions are ones that are easy and cheap for you to make, but that are of high value to the other party. For example, unused office space and results of pre-existing research are two ideal concessions at Lucinda's disposal. They won't place any financial burden on her organization but both address pressing problems that Mabel's company is battling to solve.

Question

Frank and Danny are meeting to discuss how Frank's IT solutions company can help Danny's company develop software for its financial planners to help them access key market figures and competitive intelligence. They are currently in the value exchange phase of their sales meeting.

Which are appropriate concessions for Frank to offer during the value-exchange stage of the meeting?

Options:

1. Product training for the employees at Danny's organization

2. 24/7 technical support

3. Quarterly review and improvement of the software

4. Free use of his company's conference facilities

Answer

Option 1: This option is correct. Providing training is unlikely to place a heavy financial burden on Frank's company, which already has the needed staff and expertise to do this. Offering to do this also demonstrates concern that the product will have real benefit for Danny's organization.

Option 2: This is a correct option. Frank's company already has a center for providing clients with full- time technical support. So technical support will be inexpensive for Frank to provide but of potentially high value to Danny's company.

Option 3: This is an incorrect option. Although Frank's company may have the staff and expertise to offer quarterly updates to the software, this could end up being a commitment that robs the company of many billable production hours.

Option 4: This option is incorrect. This concession lacks any real business value because it doesn't tie in with a particular need that Danny's organization has.

SECTION 2 - WHEN TO OFFER CONCESSIONS

SECTION 2 - When to Offer Concessions

To be an effective sales negotiator, you need to know when to stand your ground and when to offer concessions. You have to be patient and act strategically if you're to secure the best deal. This involves following three guidelines – don't be the first to make concessions, trade concessions gradually, and start with small concessions early on and increase concession size later.

BEST PRACTICES FOR OFFERING CONCESSIONS

Best practices for offering concessions

The ancient Greek poet Hesiod once said, "Observe due measure, for right timing is in all things the most important factor." When it comes to effective sales negotiations, the same can be said. Timing is critical. You need to know when to stand firm and when to give ground by offering concessions. So it's not just what concessions you have to offer that's relevant – it's also when you offer them that affects your success in a sales negotiation.

Negotiation is a strategic process that requires effective tactics. Although situations differ, following three general guidelines about when to trade concessions can help you succeed:
- don't be the first to make concessions,
- trade concessions gradually, and
- start with small concessions and make larger ones later on.

Negotiation Skills for Sales Professionals

In reflecting on prior negotiations, you may have noted that offering a concession first can come across as a sign of weakness – especially if you accidentally offer it too early. It's the right time to offer a concession only when the other party is about to stop negotiating and considering your terms. But it can be difficult to tell when this time has arrived.

For example, the other party may be outwardly resisting your initial proposal but actually expecting to have to agree to elements of it. Or the other party may be thinking about what else to offer you to secure your agreement to particular terms.

If you then jump in and offer a concession, it may be taken as a sign of weakness. It suggests you might be willing to give more concessions if the other party just does its best to hold out.

The solution is to avoid being the first one to offer a concession. If the other party has already agreed to give ground, you can also do so when necessary – without the risk of appearing weak.

However, if you have to go first because the other party really won't give way, make sure your first concession is minor. An ideal concession has only a small impact for your side but is relatively valuable to the other party.

It's important to be patient when negotiating – and particularly when offering concessions. In an effort to wrap negotiations up quickly, it can be tempting to rush things by offering many of your concessions early on. You may believe that presenting numerous concessions all at once will dazzle the other party and make things easier. But that's unlikely.

If you give too many concessions too soon, it can put you at a significant disadvantage. It's likely you'll have made unnecessary concessions. It also means you'll have used up your most valuable bargaining tools. You'll then have little room left to maneuver.

Made unnecessary concessions

Say you're negotiating the sale of a fleet of vehicles to another company. You try to complete negotiations quickly by offering a 7% discount plus 2 free vehicles. These are among the major concessions you determined you're willing to make when planning for the negotiation.

The purchaser is actually willing to settle for just the discount. So by offering too much too soon, you've given away vehicles you didn't need to.

Used up bargaining tools

You're negotiating the sale of 20 new computers. To avoid wasting time with haggling over prices, the buyer resorts to her worst-case scenario – she offers to purchase additional software with the computers and agrees to pay 90% of the sale price. You pick up on this urgency and reject the offer, hoping to squeeze more out of the deal.

By offering all her major concessions all at once, the buyer makes subsequent negotiation very difficult because you're now in a position of strength. To continue with the negotiation, she would need to offer further concessions – each of which would cause her to go beyond the limits she set before the negotiation.

To avoid these problems, it's best to take your time and trade concessions gradually. For example, you may offer one concession at a time, as and when necessary. Or you may gradually increase the value of a particular concession – such as a discount – up to the maximum value you decided before the meeting. If both sides take this step-by-step approach, it helps manage the pace of negotiation in a way that leads to a more reasonable compromise.

During the preparation phase, you should already have ranked the concessions you're willing to offer – so you'll know which ones are of primary and secondary importance, based on how valuable they are.

This is important when it comes to determining when to offer each of your concessions.

If your opening concessions are big, the other party could develop high expectations of you – anticipating that your subsequent concessions will also be big.

For this reason, it's better to start small – offer secondary concessions at the beginning. You can then build up the perception that you're willing to concede on some of your demands for the sake of agreement.

As negotiation continues, you can offer some of the more valuable concessions you prepared if it proves necessary to do this.

PUTTING THE BEST PRACTICES IN ACTION

Putting the best practices in action

Lucinda is about to meet with Mabel to negotiate a deal in which Lucinda's high-tech consultancy helps Mabel's wireless device company with marketing counsel and with the design and interoperability of its devices. Lucinda has prepared for the meeting by deciding on a negotiation plan that includes what concessions she can offer and when.

Follow along as Lucinda and Mabel try to come to an agreement.

Lucinda: Given our track record and the benefits you stand to gain from our service, I've calculated that we'll need $140,000 in fees to do the work.

Mabel: Financially, we're in a tight spot, so that kind of figure isn't feasible. My friend Chelsea said you did the same job for her company for only $95,000. Can't you match that price, given my situation?

Lucinda: Chelsea's company was in much better shape – it didn't have the negative media attention and technical issues that you do. In your case, there's more work to be done to repair and rebuild your brand, and that takes time and money. If you don't act now, imagine how much worse things could get...

Mabel: That's true...but it's still high. If we drop marketing services from the deal, would $100,000 do it for you? I need maximum value from this deal.

Lucinda: You've closed offices in Manchester and Stockholm recently, haven't you? I could throw in the free use of our office space in those places, along with some basic services like phones and administrative support.

Mabel: Thanks. Yes, that would help us out in terms of international business. But $140,000 is still too much. How about $110,000? And I'll throw in five of our brand new wireless devices every six months.

Lucinda: The devices sound good, but I can't settle for that price.

Lucinda: Look – you're struggling with interoperability issues. We have some very useful research that could mean a big boost to your product development. I can give you that too. My absolute final offer on the price is $125,000.

Mabel: It's still a little high, but the extras you're offering could be very valuable to our bottom line. So...yes, we have a deal!

In this negotiation, Lucinda followed three best practices for offering concessions. Select each best practice to learn how Lucinda implemented it.

Don't be first

Lucinda didn't offer the first concession. She stuck to her original price and waited for Mabel to offer $100,000 before she offered her first concession – international office space and services.

Trade gradually

Lucinda didn't offer all her concessions at once. She traded her concessions gradually, first offering office space and services, and then, after receiving a counter-concession, adding the research and price discount.

Start small

Lucinda made her small concession early and offered the larger concessions later. She started by offering Mabel's company use of free office space and research findings, and ended with a price discount – which was the biggest concession of the three.

Question

Frank – a senior business analyst – is meeting with Danny to discuss the provision of consulting services for a software development project that Danny's financial company is undertaking.

Which actions demonstrate the use of best practices for when to offer concessions?

Options:

1. He offers 24/7 support first, then free advertising

2. Frank opens the negotiations by agreeing to a six-week time frame

3. He saves the price discount until the later stages of negotiation

4. He starts bargaining by offering a discount first so Danny knows his intentions are good

5. He only softens his stance after Danny raises his offer to $132,000

Answer

Option 1: This option is correct. Frank trades his concessions gradually – one at a time. And then later, when even this isn't enough, he adds yet another concession in the form of a price discount.

Option 2: This is an incorrect option. Frank doesn't make the first concession. He waits for Danny to concede first – with a price increase – before he offers his first concession of user support.

Option 3: This is a correct option. Frank starts by offering a small concession – user support. He also adds a more valuable concession – free advertising. He then offers his largest and final concession – the discount.

Option 4: This option is incorrect. Frank offers the biggest concession – the discount – only at the end of negotiations. He starts bargaining by offering smaller concessions first – user support and advertising.

Option 5: This option is correct. Frank doesn't offer the first concession – he waits for Danny to do so. After Danny raises the price to $132,000, Frank offers his first concession – 24/7 on-hand support.

SECTION 3 - HOW TO OFFER CONCESSIONS

SECTION 3 - How to Offer Concessions

In a sales negotiation, you can use concessions effectively by ensuring the other party knows you expect something in return, making the concessions in installments, and emphasizing the value of your concessions while minimizing the value of those you're offered in return. This can help ensure you secure the best deal possible.

OFFERING CONCESSIONS EFFECTIVELY

Offering concessions effectively

It's not always what you offer, or when you offer, but how you offer it that makes a difference. When you're negotiating a sale, you can use three strategies to make sure your concessions are effective in securing a good deal. You can make sure other parties know you expect reciprocity, make concessions in installments, and emphasize the value of your concessions while minimizing the value of theirs.

EXPECTING RECIPROCITY

Expecting reciprocity

When you're negotiating and you make a concession, you should subtly demand a return for what you've offered. To ensure your negotiation partner will reciprocate your concessions, you first need to define your concession, then request reciprocation, and finally suggest what concession you'd like in return.

1. Define your concession

The first step is to define your concession – or what you're willing to give up – clearly.

For example, you might say something like "What if my company offered you free technical support, 24 hours a day?" Using wording like "what if" immediately makes it clear you're proposing a concession provided you're offered something in return.

2. Request reciprocation

Once you've defined your concession, you should make it clear that you expect a concession from the other party in return.

For example, you might ask a direct question like "So what can you offer in return?" Alternatively, if you used phrasing like "What if" to describe the concession you're offering, you might simply pause and wait for the other party to reciprocate.

3. Suggest form of concession

When requesting reciprocation, you can indicate the type of concession you want the other party to make.

For example, you might follow up a proposal that your company provides technical support with a suggestion such as "In return, can your company commit to a five-year contract?"

Take Lucinda and Mabel. Lucinda is asking a price of $125,000 for her company's services, but Mabel isn't ready to accept this price. If they're to reach an agreement, Lucinda and Mabel will need to make concessions.

Follow along as Lucinda and Mabel each make concessions and ensure they get something in return.

Mabel: I'm sorry, but we simply can't pay $125,000. The company has already had to close a number of its satellite offices in other countries as a result of the financial strain.

Lucinda: Well, we have international offices with free space in two of the countries you trade in. What if your executives made use of that space?

Mabel: That sounds good.

Lucinda: It will save your company a lot of money. You can avoid the high rental prices and the need to enter any long-term leases.

Mabel: Yes, I agree. Still, $125,000 is rather high.

Lucinda: OK. What if my company were to offer the use of its administrative services too? That would also save you money. Are you now able to rethink my asking price?

Mabel: Yes, you have a good point.

Lucinda defines her concessions and emphasizes they will save Mabel's company money. She then asks directly for a reciprocal concession from Mabel. As a result, Mabel reconsiders Lucinda's asking price. By using wording like "what if," Lucinda implies that she expects something in return for the concession she's offering.

OFFERING IN INSTALLMENTS

Offering in installments

Offering concessions in installments – either one at a time or by gradually increasing the value of an initial concession you offer – can have several benefits. It emphasizes the value of the concessions you offer, encourages further negotiation, and shows you're flexible.

Highlights value of concessions

If you offer concessions in installments, your concessions seem more valuable and are therefore appreciated. Each installment shows you're willing to negotiate and meet the needs or wants of the other party.

For example, you know you could offer a client a 10% discount. You could start by offering a 5% discount and, later in the conversation, increase the offer to a 10% discount.

Encourages further negotiation

Offering concessions in installments gives you more to negotiate with and makes it likely you'll be offered more in return.

For example, you can ask for a particular concession in return for a 5% discount – and later on, request a second concession in return for increasing the discount to 10%.

Shows you're flexible

With each successive concession you offer, you demonstrate you're willing to listen and react to the other party's needs. This makes it more likely that the other party will reciprocate by trying to meet your needs.

Lucinda decides in advance what concessions she's able to offer. Mabel is resistant to accept the initial asking price, so Lucinda first highlights some of the issues Mabel's company has to overcome. Only after more resistance from Mabel does Lucinda offer a small concession – the use of office space. By offering her concession in installments, Lucinda ensures she doesn't give away too much too quickly in order to achieve the best deal possible.

VALUING CONCESSIONS

Valuing concessions

A final strategy is to emphasize the value of your concessions while minimizing the value of the other party's concessions. To do this, you can detail the cost to you of providing a concession, emphasize the benefits it will have for the other party, and avoid appearing overly impressed with what you're offered in return.

Detail cost to you

Whenever possible, you should stress what a concession you offer will cost you or your company. The cost you point to may be financial or relate to time and resources. It could also relate to other missed opportunities or risks your company will be assuming.

Sometimes using a statement such as "This won't be easy for us" before stating what your company can offer can also help emphasize the value of a concession.

Emphasize benefits

As well as outlining what a concession will cost you, you should emphasize how it will benefit the other party.

For example, if you're offering an administrative service, you can explain how it will save a company time and money.

Avoid appearing impressed

Even when the other party offers you a reciprocal concession that you're very happy with, you shouldn't seem overly keen.

Your reactions should suggest that the other party is getting the better deal because you're giving up something you initially demanded. This may encourage the other party to offer further concessions or to conclude an agreement.

Follow along as Lucinda outlines the cost of her concessions to her company and how Mabel will benefit from accepting those concessions.

Mabel: I agree that the use of administrative services as well as office space will save my company money, but I'm still not sure of the asking price.

Lucinda: We're going to have to undertake a significant amount of rebuilding and repositioning of your company brand before we even think about embarking on more promotions. This is costly and time consuming, so we do need to stick to the budget of $125,000.

Mabel: You have a good point, but I'm concerned, as we simply can't afford it.

Lucinda: Well, the use of office space will benefit you due to the recent office closures your company has had to make. It will also save your company a lot of money as rental prices can be high and it will help you avoid entering any long-term lease agreements.

Lucinda emphasizes the cost of helping Mabel's company and uses it to support her resistance to dropping the price.

She highlights the benefits of her concessions by explaining they will save Mabel's company a lot of money.

By defining the cost, being resistant, and highlighting the benefits of her concessions, Lucinda persuades Mabel to reconsider her asking price.

PUTTING IT ALL TOGETHER

Putting it all together
  Case Study: Question 1 of 2
  Scenario

Frank, a senior business analyst for an IT solutions organization, is meeting Danny to negotiate a deal for developing software for financial planners at Danny's company. Frank notices he needs to start offering concessions if the deal is to survive.

Answer the question in any order.

Question

Frank and Danny are going to negotiate the price and the completion schedule for the new project.

Which statements should Frank use to present his concessions?

Options:

1. "What if we agree to deliver the software two weeks earlier?"

2. "If we deliver earlier, you'll be able to get the product out in time for the start of the next financial year."

3. "The cost you're proposing is too little. The amount of work we'll have to do is greatly increased as a result of having to rebuild your company's reputation."

4. "Yes, it will be wonderful if your company agrees to give us more business – we'll definitely lower our price then!"

5. "We can help you, but we won't accept less than the asking price."

Answer

Option 1: This option is correct. Frank uses the words "what if" to offer a specific concession and to indicate that he expects something in return.

Option 2: This is a correct option. Frank emphasizes the value of the concession he offers by explaining how it will benefit Danny's company.

Option 3: This option is correct. Frank emphasizes the value of what he's offering by detailing the cost to his company and therefore minimizing Danny's concession.

Option 4: This is an incorrect option. Frank should be careful not to appear overly impressed by the concessions that Danny offers. He should minimize the value he assigns to them, or it's likely he'll end up with a worse deal than he could have secured.

Option 5: This option is incorrect. You want to be resistant, but you shouldn't be completely unwilling to negotiate.

Case Study: Question 2 of 2

Frank decides in advance that the lowest price he can offer Danny's company is $130,000. He can also offer the company 24-hour support for users of the software and free advertising on his company's web site.

Which is the best way for Frank to offer his concessions?

Options:

1. Tell Danny everything he has to offer – including the lowest price and the other concessions he can make – and then ask Danny what he can do in return

2. Open by asking for $145,000, add other concessions if he can't persuade Danny, and gradually drop the price only if necessary

3. Open with an offer for $130,000 and make additional concessions – like the 24-hour support and free advertising – only if Danny doesn't agree to this price

Answer

Option 1: This option is incorrect. By telling Danny everything he has to offer, Frank may be giving away more than he needs to and leaving himself with nothing further to negotiate with. Instead he should make his concessions in installments.

Option 2: This is the correct option. Frank should make his concessions in installments and only as they prove necessary. He's likely to secure a much better deal in return if he does this.

Option 3: This is an incorrect option. Frank shouldn't open with the lowest price he'll accept. He'll appear inflexible if he then refuses to drop the price further.

CHAPTER 3 - REACHING AGREEMENT

CHAPTER 3 - Reaching Agreement
   SECTION 1 - Instilling Trust during a Sales Negotiation
   SECTION 2 - Countering Negotiation Tactics
   SECTION 3 - Overcoming Barriers during a Sales Meeting

SECTION 1 - INSTILLING TRUST DURING A SALES NEGOTIATION

SECTION 1 - Instilling Trust during a Sales Negotiation

Trust is a vital component of sales negotiation – a lack of trust can block a deal even if you're offering fantastic value to a client.

To instill trust in a client, you need to do more than being sincere and reliable. You can express empathy with the client, you can provide adequate documentation to back up your product and reputation, you can emphasize the value you place on a lasting business relationship with a client above a quick profit, and you can ensure transparency.

STRATEGIES FOR INSTILLING TRUST

Strategies for instilling trust

The decision about whether to buy a product or service often comes down to trust. For example, you compare prices of an identical vehicle at ten different dealerships. As you discuss the vehicle with each salesperson, you may ask yourself "Would I buy a vehicle from this person?" The question makes an important point. Based on the behavior of the salespersons, you rule out five deals, despite their competitive prices. You're more likely to take your business to a salesperson who comes across as trustworthy.

So trust is vital for successful sales negotiations. If people trust you, they'll be confident that you'll work with them to secure a mutually beneficial agreement – rather than to benefit yourself at their expense.

There are two forms of trust that are important to sales negotiations – trust gained from prior knowledge of a person or organization, or trust given on a hunch in the absence of such knowledge.

Negotiations that take place between trusting parties are characterized by a free and honest exchange of information. As a result, the negotiations are generally quicker and more efficient. Trust often negates the need to battle over every single point of a contract and certainly involves less legal wrangling.

If you're considered untrustworthy, it can have a negative effect on your ability to conclude sales in two main ways. It can limit your access to information and, more directly, prevent customers from giving you their business.

Limit access to information

If potential customers don't trust you, they'll be hesitant to give up any information for fear that you could use it to your advantage and to their detriment.

This means you may not get the information you require to understand your customers' needs. In turn, this will severely hamper your ability to negotiate effectively. You won't know what is and is not important to the customers, and so you won't be able to offer attractive concessions or solutions.

Prevent customers from giving you business

If you're perceived as untrustworthy or unfair, a deal you propose will probably be regarded in the same way. So it's likely that customers will choose not to deal with you, even if they stand to gain from doing so.

Similarly, if you appear untrustworthy at any stage during a negotiation, a customer may simply walk away from a potential deal.

Question

You may know you're trustworthy and have customers' interests at heart, but why is it important that customers really do trust you?

Options:

1. They're more likely to give you the information you need to fully understand their needs

2. They won't be suspicious about the value of the deal you're proposing, thinking there's a hidden catch

3. They're more likely to spend beyond what their budgets will allow

4. If the first deal is positive for them, they won't feel the need to negotiate with you over future deals

Answer

Option 1: This option is correct. If customers don't trust you, they may withhold information from you for fear that you may use it to your advantage.

Option 2: This is a correct option. Even if you're offering customers a good deal, they may think you're hiding something if you appear untrustworthy.

Option 3: This is an incorrect option. Merely being trustworthy won't convince customers to spend more money than they have.

Option 4: This option is incorrect. Customers may negotiate for a better deal even if they trust you, simply due to the nature of business.

To appear trustworthy, you need to either display the necessary personality traits – sincerity, integrity, and fairness, or be known to act in a trustworthy manner in your business dealings. The best strategies for instilling trust in a customer are to express empathy, provide documentation to back up your claims, explain the value of a shared business relationship, and assure the customer of transparency.

Express empathy

To express empathy, you need to make it clear you understand the customer's perspective and the business challenges they are up against. This may not change the values of the items being exchanged, but it will help you earn the customer's trust.

Provide documentation

If you're able, provide documentation to verify your claims about pricing and market value, your company's track record, the terms of the proposed deal, and your scope for negotiation. It's important the documentation is genuine and credible, otherwise people may dismiss it as additional baseless advertising.

Value the relationship

You can explain you value a lasting business relationship with the customer over the opportunity to make a quick one-off sale. By explaining this relationship depends on the satisfactory outcome of the negotiation, you can exert some pressure.

Assure transparency

If you provide your customers with transparency and access to supervise the work in progress, they can verify that you're fulfilling your side of the deal.

Consider a manufacturer who brokers a deal with a distributor who'll sell their cell phone cases. The distributor provides transparency by allowing the manufacturer to regularly examine the financial records associated with the deal. That way, the manufacturer knows the company is being paid as per agreement for goods sold.

To observe a sales professional using these techniques, take the example of Lucinda, who works as a sales lead for a multinational high-tech consultancy. She's just confirmed a meeting with Mabel, the vice president of development at an established wireless device company.

While preparing for the meeting, Lucinda discovers that the company has recently experienced problems with its wireless device development. It's also been the focus of several very negative news articles after some of its devices proved to be inoperable on certain computer platforms.

Mindful of this, she determines the approximate cost of providing the services Mabel wants, for a one- year period, would be approximately $125,000. To turn a decent profit, she would like to ask Mabel for $140,000.

As a first step, Lucinda ensures when she draws up a meeting agenda, she leaves some free time at the start of the meeting for personal introductions and socializing. This helps put Mabel at ease and provides a good starting point to start building a trusting relationship.

Lucinda: Now let's get down to business! I think my company has the skills and technology to help you.

Mabel: I approached your company due to the experience you have in this area, but you must realize we're facing a few very special problems.

Lucinda: Well, I've been doing some research and I have an idea how we can adapt our previous approaches to suit your company's needs. Here's the documentation I put together.

Mabel: OK...this looks promising.

Lucinda: I know you're facing some nasty problems – we were in a similar situation a few years back. But even if the issues seem daunting, we can overcome them with the right approach.

Mabel: Thanks, yes – I hope so.

In the opening part of the negotiation, Lucinda uses two strategies to help win Mabel's trust – she does express empathy and provides documentation to strengthen her claims.

Express empathy

In order to express empathy, Lucinda makes it clear she understands the problems Mabel's organization is facing by referring to similar problems from her own past.

Provide documentation

To allay Mabel's doubts, Lucinda uses documentation to show how her company's existing technology and expertise can be adapted to suit the needs of Mabel's company.

The documentation shows that Lucinda's assurances are more than just a slick sales pitch. She's invested time and effort in considering the customer's requirements. This builds trust.

Lucinda and Mabel continue with the meeting. Lucinda presents an opening offer of $140,000 for the services she's determined that Mabel's company needs. Mabel immediately says she knows that Lucinda's company performed similar services for another company at a cost of $95,000.

Lucinda realizes this may be an obstacle to getting the deal signed, and that the trust between her and Mabel is in danger.

Follow along as Lucinda and Mabel continue discussing the deal.

Lucinda: I realize that in comparison to the deal you mentioned, the $140,000 price tag seems steep. But your company is facing those interoperability issues which will require us to put in more work.

Mabel: Unfortunately our budget is limited to $100,000 and I just don't understand how the difference between the deals warrants such a huge price jump.

Lucinda: If you check the documentation I gave you, you'll notice the cost calculations for the work required to resolve those interoperability issues. This work wasn't included in the $95,000 deal.

Lucinda: I know those issues are a real problem for your company. I'd like to work together to resolve them. I believe this work will foster a strong relationship between our two companies, for now and in the future.

Mabel: Our budget is tight and these problems need to be sorted out quickly! Lucinda: I'll get my best people to make it a top priority! It'll be in our best interests to ensure this deal works for you.

Mabel: It's a lot of complicated work...

Lucinda: We'll make it work. You're welcome to supervise the work in progress and I'll have our team work closely with your people.

Mabel: That is reassuring. Thanks Lucinda!

When a disagreement arises in the negotiation, Lucinda knows she needs to do more to cultivate Mabel's trust. So she explains the value she places on the relationship between the two companies and assures Mabel full transparency.

Explain the value of a relationship

By emphasizing the value she places on a mutually beneficial business relationship, Lucinda assures Mabel that her company can be trusted – it isn't after a quick, one-off deal.

Assure transparency

Lucinda offers Mabel full transparency by inviting Mabel to supervise her company's work and promising that her team will work closely with Mabel's team. So Mabel will be able to observe the work as it's done to ensure all promises are kept.

Because Lucinda uses the strategies to earn Mabel's trust, she succeeds in negotiating a deal that's beneficial to both parties. The increased trust also means there's a greater possibility that the companies will work together in the future and develop a lasting business relationship.

Question

Frank and Danny's companies worked successfully together on several software projects in the pasts. During their last project, however, Danny's company had to spend more money to fix several errors Frank's company introduced, which resulted in a loss of revenue. Frank and Danny are currently negotiating a new deal when a disagreement arises over Frank's price of $147, 000. Danny recalls the errors his company previously had to fix and threatens to end the negotiation.

Which are examples of appropriate ways for Frank to regain Danny's trust and so successfully complete the negotiation?

Options:

1. Present product test reports to prove the new software works better than the previous package

2. Explain the new software will have more features than the previous packages his company designed

3. Assure Danny the existing relationship between the two companies is his top priority

4. Advise Danny he's unlikely to find a better deal elsewhere and refuse to budge on the original price

5. Say he understands Danny's reluctance, but continued negotiation could still yield beneficial results

6. Offer to allow Danny's IT team to periodically review the software during development

Answer

Option 1: This is a correct option. Presenting Danny with documentation to back up claims that past errors have been fixed is a good way to regain Danny's trust.

Option 2: This option is incorrect. The product's extra features aren't directly relevant at this point in the negotiation. Failing to address the cause of Danny's mistrust could lead to Danny stopping negotiations.

Option 3: This option is correct. Frank can help instill trust in Danny by prioritizing the value he places on the relationship between their companies.

Option 4: This is an incorrect option. By challenging his opinion, Frank's likely to reinforce Danny's mistrust. Danny may then end the negotiation before a deal is struck.

Option 5: This is a correct option. By expressing empathy, Frank demonstrates he's considering Danny's situation and perspective – rather than just his own. This is likely to increase Danny's trust in him.

Option 6: This is a correct option. By being transparent to Danny, Frank can allay any of Danny's fears that the software may contain errors.

SECTION 2 - COUNTERING NEGOTIATION TACTICS

SECTION 2 - Countering Negotiation Tactics

To handle sales negotiations effectively, you have to know how to counter the tactics that customers use to try to win the negotiations. The two most commonly used tactics are the "no deal" and anchoring techniques.

You can counter the no-deal tactic by showing the customer why your offer is reasonable, pointing out how it differs from competing offers and why it provides better value. You can counter the anchoring technique by shifting the focus away from the extreme offer a customer makes. You illustrate to the customer how your company can add value and you hold firm to your price.

RESPONDING TO NEGOTIATION TACTICS

Responding to negotiation tactics

It's a scenario you've probably experienced often. You're sitting down at the table with your customer, both of you trying to find the best value for your companies. You suggest a price. Your customer knows it's a cheaper price than a competitor would offer. However, she acts outraged and threatens to leave if you don't offer a lower price. How do you counter tactics like these?

In a sales negotiation, you can count on the other party trying to use various tactics to win the best deal. If you're unprepared for these tactics, you may be manipulated into conceding too much and find yourself on the losing end of a deal.

Two of the tactics that customers use most often are the "no-deal" tactic – or claiming they can do better if they don't make a deal with you, and using an anchoring tactic, called hard bargaining, that's designed to force you to lower your price. Other examples of tactics are using put-downs, concealing information, making last-minute demands, and asking for free concessions.

The no-deal tactic

Customers may try to force you to accept a worse deal by claiming they can do better by walking away and either making a deal with someone else or taking an alternative course of action.

For example, customers may give an exaggerated reaction to a price offer you make, claiming they can get the same services for half the price from your competitors – even if there's little or no basis for this claim.

Anchoring tactic

An anchor point is a chosen starting point on which the negotiations are based. In this technique, the customer makes an extreme offer with the expectation that the seller will try bring the offer down to a compromise or acceptable midpoint. Typically, the compromise is still higher than the seller had intended to agree to when planning objectives. Hard bargaining is an example of an anchoring tactic.

Hard bargaining

Customers who use hard bargaining usually do so as part of the anchoring tactic. They try to fight for every bit of value they can get around an anchoring point. They may corner you into giving concessions beyond those you originally planned to offer.

Hard bargaining is an aggressive and often confrontational type of negotiating tactic. It involves bluffing, posturing, and pressuring the other party in an attempt to win the best deal.

Using put-downs

Put-downs are a way of dominating a negotiation by undermining the confidence of the other party. By being derogatory about a proposal, or about your ability to secure a deal, the other party tries to lower your aspirations – so that you offer more and expect less in return.

Concealing information

Customers may keep potentially deal-changing information about their demands to themselves, while inviting you to disclose all your demands.

Making last-minute demands

Last-minute demands are designed to throw you off balance. The theory is you'll be more inclined to concede to these demands because you're close to closing the deal.

Asking for concessions

Customers may try to get any concessions possible – for example, by asking you to lower your prices or throw in something for free.

Say you offer to sell a customer factory equipment at a price of $100,000. The customer immediately acts shocked, saying the price is outrageous and the same equipment is available elsewhere at nearly half the price. Secretly though, the customer doesn't believe your price is all that high. In this example, the customer is using the no-deal tactic – claiming that an alternative to making a deal with you will provide much better value.

Now suppose you're offering a customer a discount of 20% on networking equipment. The customer immediately demands a discount of at least 40% and a favorable service contract. As you continue negotiating, the customer uses every possible opportunity to pressure you into giving further concessions. This is an example of hard bargaining.

Question

You're negotiating the cost of updating a customer's network architecture. You state a price of $170,000. The customer says that's too expensive and prepares to leave – secretly expecting you to immediately offer a much lower price.

Which type of negotiation tactic is the customer using?

Options:

1. The no-deal tactic
2. Hard bargaining
3. Put-downs
4. Asking for last-minute concessions

Answer

Option 1: This is the correct option. The customer is threatening to walk away from the deal as a tactic to make you lower your price. So this is an example of using the no-deal tactic.

Option 2: This is an incorrect option. The customer in this case isn't consistently trying to bully more and more concessions from you. Instead, the customer is threatening to walk out on the deal.

Option 3: This is an incorrect option. The customer in this case doesn't belittle you in an attempt to lower your expectations of the deal. Instead, the customer threatens to end the negotiation.

Option 4: This is an incorrect option. The customer in this example threatens to end the negotiation prematurely, rather than asking for concessions just before an agreement is finalized.

To be the best sales negotiator, you need to recognize the negotiation tactics your customers use and know how to counter these tactics.

The no-deal tactic is all too common, but you can counter it effectively. If a customer threatens to walk out on you, claiming that competitors offer lower prices, you can calmly show why your offer is reasonable. If relevant, you can also explain how other offers differ from yours and why yours represents better value. Finally, you should know when it's appropriate to lower your price.

Show your offer is reasonable

You should respond to a customer's outburst by keeping calm and objective, and demonstrating why your offer is reasonable.

For example, you could use your calculator to show the customer exactly how you arrived at the price you've offered, given factors like your expenses and time constraints. This shows the customer you've considered your price carefully and don't easily lose your composure.

Explain how others differ

If a customer quotes an offer available from a competitor, you can point out how it differs from your offer – explaining why it can't be compared and why your offer is a better proposition.

For example, you might point out limitations or hidden disadvantages of a competitor's package and explain that unlike that package, yours comes with a service contract.

Know when to lower your price

If a competitor is genuinely offering a customer better value than you are, it may be time to consider lowering your price.

Lucinda is the sales lead for a high-tech consultancy. She's meeting with Mabel, the vice president of a wireless devices company, to negotiate her fee for a planned project.

Follow along as Lucinda counters Mabel's use of the no-deal tactic.

Lucinda: We can help you restore your company's status as leader in the field of wireless devices for the sum of $140,000.

Mabel: Outrageous! I can get a much better price from at least three other companies!

Lucinda: Perhaps, but ask yourself if any other company can draw on the kind of high-tech expertise that we can. We can improve the interoperability of your devices, align your marketing with best practices, and make you the number one player in the industry.

Mabel: The price is too high.

Lucinda: We're basing this figure on previous work done for some major players, for which we asked $120,000 each, as well as the consultancy work over the year which comes to another $20,000. Please remember not only will we be helping out with your technology needs, we'll also be giving input into some of your marketing functions.

In the scenario, Lucinda stays calm when Mabel threatens to walk out. Instead of giving in to the demand to drop her price, she points out how her offer differs from the ones available from competitors.

She then calculates costs to show Mabel she's used a reasonable process to arrive at her asking price.

Question

Frank is negotiating the sale of business consultancy services to Danny, who represents a financial planning organization. Danny immediately rejects the price Frank offers, comparing it to a competitor's price and threatening to leave the meeting.

In which ways should Frank respond?

Options:

1. Save the negotiation by apologizing and changing his price to suit Danny

2. Point out how his offer differs from that of the competitor

3. Demonstrate to Danny how he arrived at the price

4. Act offended and let Danny leave, expecting him to return once he's realized he's made a mistake

5. Be willing to lower his price if the competitor's offer really is better than his

Answer

Option 1: This is an incorrect option. This is exactly what Danny wants – to force concessions out of Frank. Instead, Frank should remain calm and show Danny why his price is reasonable.

Option 2: This is a correct option. Frank recognizes the no-deal tactic and shows why his price is different from others.

Option 3: This is a correct option. Frank notices the tactic and clearly shows how he reached his price so there's no room for misunderstanding or suspicion.

Option 4: This is an incorrect option. Once Danny has reached the point of walking away, he won't return to the negotiation.

Option 5: This is a correct option. Frank should concede if it is absolutely necessary to do so.

To counter an anchoring tactic, you should redirect the discussion away from the extreme offer or demand a customer has made. You shouldn't acknowledge the offer or demand in any way, or you're trapped into using it as the negotiation's starting point. After you've successfully redirected the conversation, you restate your asking price – based on what you planned instead of in reaction to the customer's proposal.

Lucinda and Mabel are negotiating the price of consultancy services. Mabel says her company is under financial strain and she can't pay more than $60,000. Lucinda has planned on charging her $140,000 but by anchoring on a figure and citing financial pressure, Mabel makes this more difficult for her.

Mabel: I was thinking along the lines of $60,000...

Lucinda: We have the perfect team for this kind of job – a balance between business and technical expertise.

Mabel: That's good. The right team is important.

Lucinda: Yes, and our team can help you reach even higher profit margins. Not only will we work on a new brand image that will capture a larger market share, we'll also sort out the interoperability problems your flagship product is currently experiencing. We can give you this, plus unlimited use of our office space. So $140,000 is quite reasonable.

When faced with a seemingly nonnegotiable starting offer, Lucinda recognizes the anchoring technique and doesn't begin compromising her planned objective. Instead, she first redirects the conversation, emphasizing the value in her offer, and then restates her asking price.

In this way, she moves the main point of negotiation away from Mabel and into her own hands.

Question

Danny offers Frank an outrageously low fee of $90,000 for Frank's business consultancy services, $40,000 less than Frank's offer.

In which ways can Frank counter this tactic?

Options:

1. Tell Danny he can't possibly go lower than $95,000
2. Tell Danny he understands but charge him $94,000
3. Tell Danny he can identify ways of improving the profitability of his business
4. Demonstrate to Danny how he arrived at the price of $130,000

Answer

Option 1: This is an incorrect option. Frank shouldn't lower his price at this stage unless his offer is really too high. If Frank suggests a lower price, then that will be the price Danny will use as a starting point for negotiation.

Option 2: This is an incorrect option. Danny wants to set the tone with a demand and Frank shouldn't acknowledge it in any way.

Option 3: This is a correct option. Recognizing the tactic, Frank chooses to redirect the conversation without acknowledging Danny's demand.

Option 4: This is a correct option. Frank identifies the tactic Danny is using. Without giving in, he demonstrates why his offer of $130,000 is reasonable.

SECTION 3 - OVERCOMING BARRIERS DURING A SALES MEETING

SECTION 3 - Overcoming Barriers during a Sales Meeting

Lack of trust, the other party's negotiation tactics, and deadlocks are all barriers that can stall or even end sales negotiations. However, you can use specific strategies to help overcome these barriers and secure mutually beneficial agreements.

OVERCOMING NEGOTIATION BARRIERS

Overcoming negotiation barriers

Various barriers can hamper sales negotiations or prevent the parties involved from reaching a final agreement. These include a lack of trust, the various negotiation tactics that customers use to try to secure deals that favor their interests, and deadlocks – which occur when neither party can reach an agreement.

Question

You're negotiating with Simon – a real estate developer – about leasing a building to your company. During the discussion, Simon has made a number of statements that indicate he is putting up barriers and doesn't want to negotiate with you.

Match each type of negotiation barrier with the statement that exemplifies it.

Options:

A. Lack of trust
B. Negotiation tactics
C. Deadlock

Targets:

1. "Your previous landlord says you were late on the rent twice in the last year. I deal only with businesses who are punctual about payments."

2. "I'm wasting my time here. Your offer is simply ridiculous. My building is worth at least triple what you're proposing."

3. "All my tenants pay a three-month deposit on signing the lease. If you won't do that, there's no point in negotiating further."

Answer

Simon's suggesting he doesn't trust your company to make payments on time – so the issue in this example is lack of trust.

Simon's trying to use the no-deal tactic – if you don't make concessions, he'll find better value elsewhere and will walk away from the deal.

Simon's statement suggests you've both reached a deadlock – neither party can agree about the issue of the deposit.

In this book, you've learned how to overcome barriers to agreement in negotiations. In this topic, you'll be given the chance to practice the principles and strategies you've learned.

In the pages that follow, you'll need to draw on your knowledge of how to instill trust during a negotiation, how to counter commonly used negotiation tactics, and how to overcome deadlock situations.

REFERENCES

References
1. **Negotiation Skills for Rookies** - 2009, Patrick Forsyth, Cyan Communications Ltd.
2. **Strategic Negotiation: A Breakthrough 4-Step Process for Effective Business Negotiation** - 2004, Brian J. Dietmeyer and Rob Kaplan, Kaplan Professional
3. **Practical Negotiating: Tools, Tactics, & Techniques** - 2007, Tom Gosselin, John Wiley & Sons
4. **Mastering the Negotiation Process: A Practical Guide for the Healthcare Executive** - 2002, Christopher L. Laubach, Health Administration Press
5. **Global Marketing Management: Changes, Challenges and New Strategies** - 2005, Kiefer Lee and Steve Carter, Oxford University Press
6. **Mastering Business Negotiation: A Working Guide to Making Deals and**

Resolving Conflict - 2006, Roy J. Lewicki and Alexander Hiam, Jossey-Bass
7. **How to Negotiate Effectively** - 2003, David Oliver, Kogan Page
8. **Negotiation Skills for Rookies** - 2009, Patrick Forsyth, Cyan Communications
9. **Practical Negotiating: Tools, Tactics, & Techniques** - 2007, Tom Gosselin, John Wiley & Sons
10. **The Upper Hand: Winning Strategies From World-Class Negotiators** - 2006, Michael Benoliel and Linda Cashdan, Adams Media
11. **Harvard Business Essentials: Negotiation** - 2003, Harvard Business School Publishing, Harvard Business Press
12. **3-D Negotiation: Powerful Tools to Change the Game in Your Most Important Deals** - 2006, David A. Lax and James K. Sebenius, Harvard Business Press

GLOSSARY

Glossary
B

bargaining - A form of distributive negotiation. Bargaining is a simple form of negotiation process that is both competitive and positional. Bargaining predominates in one-time negotiations and often revolves around a single issue – usually price. One party usually attempts to gain advantage over another to obtain the best possible agreement.

BATNA - Abbreviation for Best Alternative to a Negotiated Agreement, the alternative action that will be taken should your proposed agreement with another party result in an unsatisfactory agreement or when an agreement fails to materialize. If the potential results of your current negotiation only offer a value that is less than your BATNA, there is no point in proceeding with the negotiation, and you should use your best available alternative option instead. Prior to the start of negotiations, each party should have ascertained its own individual BATNA.

Best Alternative to a Negotiated Agreement - See BATNA.

C

concession - Anything that you're willing to trade with another party in order to get something back that is of more value to you.

concession ranking of 1 - A concession that's ranked as 1 is a concession that's most likely to be agreed on quickly by all parties. It's a concession that you feel can be easily traded because it's of little value to you.

concession ranking of 2 - A concession that's ranked as 2 is one that isn't contentious and is unlikely to be a major point of disagreement. For this reason, it can be dealt with at a later stage of the negotiation process.

concession ranking of 3 - A concession that is of most value to you and which will lead to the most disagreement is ranked as 3. This concession is one you will want to avoid making but may have to make if all else fails.

concession strategy - A plan of the goals or positions and sometimes the underlying interests that you will be trading with the other party. Before you enter the negotiations, at the very least you should have clarity on your and the other party's goals, and a sequence of which goals you want to trade or exchange. Concession strategies vary in detail. Also called the trading plan.

currency - The agreement terms used in a negotiation to create value.

customer - An organization or person who buys products or services from another organization or person. In the context of the field sales approach, the customer refers to the decision maker who is making the decision to purchase the products or services that a field sales agent is selling to the customer or buying organization.

D

discovery time - See Q&A discussion.

dovetailing differences - Identifying differences in interests or priorities among the parties in a negotiation, and making strategic decisions based on these differences in order to create value.

N

negotiation - An interactive process between two or more parties seeking to find common ground on an issue or issues of mutual interest or dispute where the involved parties seek to make or find a mutually acceptable agreement that will be honoured by all the parties concerned.

negotiation concessions - Also sometimes referred to as trade-offs, where one or more parties to a negotiation engage in conceding, yielding, or compromising on issues under negotiation and do so either willingly or unwillingly.

negotiation meeting - Typically where most of the deal is negotiated, with most negotiation meetings being face to face between two parties – typically a buyer (customer) and a seller (salesperson).

negotiation tactics - Detailed methods employed by negotiators to gain an advantage over other parties. Tactics are often deceptive and manipulative and are used to fulfil one party's goals and objectives – often to the detriment of the other negotiation parties.

O

objective range - A range is assigned to all objectives when preparing concessions. The high range of an objective reflects a high level of expectation and is the opening offer to the other party. It should be realistic and justifiable using objective criteria and information. As negotiation takes place and concessions are made, the negotiation moves closer to your low range which represents the minimum you're willing to settle for.

objectives - The aim of strategic negotiation process, they define the desirable outcomes of and differences between participants. They remain constant, establish parties' positions, and are subject to the priorities of and concessions made during negotiation.

P

position - The official defined stance or standpoint which will be strongly defended by a negotiator. A position is usually determined by the interests of a negotiating party in the negotiation process. A position is often defined in the contract or the offer that a party puts forward or is proposing to its counterpart.

Q

Q&A discussion - Abbreviation for question and answer discussion, which takes place during the presentation stage of the sales negotiation process and is a time during which all parties can ask and answer questions about what's been discussed.

S

sales meeting - See negotiation meeting.

sales negotiation process - Used when a potential deal involves more than one variable and when both parties have something of value to exchange with one another, this four-step process comprises preparation, presentation, value exchange, and closing. It prepares the salesperson for the complexities of sales deals, improves the likelihood of reaching agreement, and facilitates lasting business relationships.

salesperson - Customer perception of one type of sales agent in the field sales approach methodology. The salesperson focuses on the customers' current levels of service.

setup - Actions away from the negotiating table that shape and reshape the situation to a negotiator's advantage. Changes in setup may include approaching the right parties to participate in the negotiation, setting the right expectations, or dealing with the right issues that engage the right set of interests.

T

trade-off - Also referred to as a concession, where one or more parties to a negotiation engage in conceding, yielding, or compromising on issues under negotiation and do so either willingly or unwillingly.

V

value creation - The result of cooperative problem-solving skills in a negotiation that uncover joint gains for both parties. Value creation is an aspect of "win-win" or "non-zero-sum" negotiation, in which both parties benefit from the agreement.

value exchange - See bargaining.

W

walk-away point - When preparing concessions, your walk-away point is any offer that falls below the low range you've set.

win-win negotiation - An integrative negotiated agreement. In theory this means the negotiating parties have reached an agreement after fully taking into account each other's interests, such that the agreement cannot be improved upon further by any other agreement. By definition, there are no resources or "money" left on the table and all creative options have been thoroughly exploited.

Z

Zone of Possible Agreement - See ZOPA.

ZOPA - Acronym for Zone of Possible Agreement, the range or area in which an agreement is satisfactory to both parties involved in the negotiation process. Often referred to as the contracting zone. ZOPA is essentially the range between each party's real base or bottom line, and is the overlap area in the low range and high range that each party is willing to pay or find acceptable in a negotiation.

www.ingramcontent.com/pod-product-compliance
Lightning Source LLC
Chambersburg PA
CBHW020921180526
45163CB00007B/2837